Pets: Mission Impossible!

Adrian Bradbury

Illustrated by Daron Parton

OXFORD
UNIVERSITY PRESS

Chapter 1

When Mr Boot got home from work he had a big smile on his face.

'Good news!' he said. 'You'll never guess what ... '

The kids loved teasing Dad.

'You're Man United's new striker?' said Archie.

'No,' said Mr Boot.

'We've all been invited for tea with the Queen?' said Martha.

'No,' said Mr Boot. 'It's even better than that. I've got a great new job ... in London!'

The children looked at each other. There were no smiles now.

'You mean – we'll have to move house?' asked Archie.

'And leave all our friends?' cried Martha.

'I'm afraid so,' said Mr Boot, looking sad. 'I thought you'd be pleased.'

The children ran straight out of the room and up the stairs. Mr and Mrs Boot heard their bedroom doors slam.

'Oh dear,' sighed Mrs Boot.

Under the dining table, the pets had been listening.

'Oh dear,' groaned Lily the dog.

'This is bad news,' agreed Buster the cat. 'We can't let this happen. Those kids will be heartbroken. They'll have to say goodbye to their friends and start a new school.'

'And we'll all have to leave this lovely
house with its big garden,' added Lily.

'We have to put our heads together and
come up with a plan,' Buster said.

'There's no point asking Bats to help though,' said Lily. She looked across the room at Bats the lizard. He never moved, except when he snapped up his dinner – a live cricket.

It was Archie who had come up with the name Bats. 'Cricket and Bats go together!' he explained.

'Yes, we don't need Bats' help,' agreed Buster. 'His name might be clever, but he isn't!'

Chapter 2

Over the next few days, Buster and Lily came up with some cunning plans. Lily refused to go for a walk. She lay still in her basket whenever Mr Boot rattled her lead. Then she whined all night, so that nobody got any sleep.

Buster sharpened his claws on the furniture – armchairs, the kitchen table, even the legs of the piano.

Bats the lizard did nothing but stand ... and watch.

'I don't know what's wrong with these pets,' complained Mrs Boot. 'They're driving me mad!'

'I think they're trying to tell us something,' said Mr Boot.

'Like what?' asked Mrs Boot.

'They're fed up with this house,' explained Mr Boot. 'They know we're about to leave and they're telling us to hurry up! What perfect timing too. The boss is coming tomorrow to sign the contract for the new job!'

'Oh no!' whispered Buster from under the table. 'That is bad news. We need all the help we can get now! Bats – that means you too!'

In his tank, Bats stood like a statue.
Had he even heard them? Only the
crickets moved, as they tried to hide under
the leaves.

Chapter 3

The next morning, everything seemed to go wrong for Mr Boot.

'Doris!' he shouted to Mrs Boot. 'What's happened to my best trousers? I can't wear them – they're covered in hairs! Have those pets been sleeping on them again?'

Downstairs, Lily and Buster winked at each other.

But Mrs Boot wasn't worried. 'Just wear your second-best suit instead. It's fine.'

Drat! Plan A had failed.

Ten minutes later, Mr Boot went to get his shoes from the cupboard in the hall.

'Doris!' wailed Mr Boot. 'What's happened to my shoes? Look at them! They're scratched to bits.'

Under the table, Buster looked at his razor-sharp claws.

But Mrs Boot wasn't worried. 'Don't make such a fuss, dear,' she said. 'We can easily hide the scratch marks with a bit of polish.'

Plan B had failed too. Oh well, Plan C would work.

Mr Boot was at the table, crunching away at his cornflakes. Suddenly, his face started to turn pale. He coughed. He gasped.

'What's the matter, darling?' asked Mrs Boot. 'Are you choking on something?'

Mrs Boot stood behind Mr Boot's chair
and gave him a big slap, right in the middle
of his back. He fell face first into his cereal
bowl. When he sat up, milk dripped from
his chin and eyelashes. He had cornflakes
stuck up both nostrils.

'Doris! What's happened to these cornflakes?' he spluttered. 'They're disgusting! They taste like dog biscuits.'

But Mrs Boot wasn't worried. 'I'll make you some toast instead,' she said. 'Calm down. We don't want anything to spoil your big day.'

Lily and Buster looked nervously at each other. Plan C had failed too. Now there was only Plan D left.

Chapter 4

Mr Boot was ready to go. He had washed the cornflakes off his face. His shoes shone.

'Bye, darling,' said Mrs Boot. 'Have a wonderful day.'

Mr Boot bent down to give her a kiss.
He stepped outside.

'Don't worry darling, I
wiiiiiiillllllaaaaarrrrrgggghhhhhhh!'

This time, Mrs Boot *was* worried.
She looked down in horror. Mr Boot
was lying at her feet.

'Darling! Are you all right?' she said.

'What happened?' groaned Mr Boot.

'You tripped over Lily,' wailed Mrs
Boot. 'One minute you were standing
and the next minute ... you weren't.'

Lily crept back into the house. She felt very mean.

'I think I need to lie down,' moaned Mr Boot.

'Nonsense,' said Mrs Boot. 'We're not going to let a little fall ruin your special day.'

At last Mr Boot was ready to leave the house. In the hall, Buster and Lily looked at each other.

'Oh well,' sighed Buster. 'We tried. We can't do anything else now.'

Chapter 5

After school, Archie and Martha stomped straight upstairs. Lily was curled up in her basket. Buster lay on the rug by the fire. There was no sign of life from the lizard tank, as usual.

Mrs Boot hummed as she made dinner. But when Mr Boot came in, she stopped. He flopped down in a chair. When he spoke, he sounded shocked.

'It was all going so well,' he said quietly. 'I met the boss. We talked about the new job in London. Then we sat down to sign the contract. I reached into my jacket pocket to get my pen ... ' He stopped.

'What happened, darling?'
asked Mrs Boot gently.

Mr Boot looked dazed.
Slowly he put his hand in
his pocket.

'When I took my pen out,
something else jumped out. It was
one of these,' he said.

He opened his fingers. In his hand
was a cricket. A live cricket.

'My whole jacket was full of crickets. They jumped out of the pockets and hopped all over the table. I pulled off my jacket and threw it away. It landed on the secretary's head. She tripped and dropped hot coffee over the boss. He jumped up and banged his head on a shelf. They had to take him to hospital. We didn't sign the contract, so I didn't get the job after all.'

Mr Boot looked at the cricket in his hand. It hopped down onto the floor and went under the sofa.

'Oh well, it's not the end of the world,' said Mrs Boot. 'Money's not everything. Just think how pleased the children will be.'

'I suppose you're right. As always. Maybe it's for the best,' sighed Mr Boot.

Lily and Buster were amazed. *Bats had his own cunning plan all along*! How had he put the crickets into Mr Boot's pocket? When?

In the lizard tank an eyelid flicked shut, then flicked open again. Was that ... a wink?

About the author

I'm from Manchester. I started my working life as a PE teacher, then was lucky enough to teach English in countries all over the world. I now split my time between writing and teaching in a primary school in Torquay. My two great passions in life are music (I annoy the neighbours by playing the piano, flute and clarinet) and all sports.

I've always liked to imagine what animals think about the world around them, especially the rather odd actions of humans. In this story I decided to see how a dog and a cat would get on if they tried to sort out a human problem. The answer: not very well!